THE STORY BEHIND

GLASS

Barbara A. Somervill

Heinemann Library
Chicago, Illinois

www.heinemannraintree.com
Visit our website to find out
more information about
Heinemann-Raintree books.

To order:
☎ Phone 888-454-2279
🖳 Visit www.heinemannraintree.com
to browse our catalog and order online.

Edited by Megan Cotugno and Diyan Leake
Designed by Philippa Jenkins
Original illustrations © Capstone Global Library Ltd.
Illustrated by Philippa Jenkins
Picture research by Hannah Taylor and Mica Brancic
Production by Eirian Griffiths
Originated by Capstone Global Library
Printed in China by CTPS

15 14 13 12 11
10 9 8 7 6 5 4 3 2 1

Library of Congress Cataloging-in-Publication Data
Somervill, Barbara A.
  The story behind glass / Barbara A. Somervill.
    p. cm.—(True stories)
  Includes bibliographical references and index.
  ISBN 978-1-4329-5437-6 (hc)
  1. Glass. I. Title.
TA450.S635 2012
666'.1—dc22   2010042102

Acknowledgments
The author and publishers are grateful to the following for
permission to reproduce copyright material:
Alamy Images p. 18 (© Westend61 GmbH); Corbis p.
8 (Werner Forman); Getty Images pp. 9 bottom (Jaron
Chubb), 13 (Science & Society); istockphoto p. 22 (©
Pgiam); Photolibrary pp. 12 (Guildhall Library & Art
Gallery), 4 (imagebroker.net/ Barbara Boensch), 24
(Imagebroker.net/ Horst Mahr); Science Photo Library
pp. 6 (Peter Menzel), 11; Shutterstock pp. 17 (© Christian
Musat), 10 (© jcpjr), iii (© Matthijs Wetterauw), 19 (©
Miroslaw Dziadkowiec), 16 (© Photobank.ch), 20 (©
PixAchi), 26 (© Simon Bratt), 23 (© Worldpics), 9 top (©
Jozef Sedmak), 25 (© Knumina), 27 (© Richard Griffin),
15 (© Royik Yevgen), 7 (© Speshilov Sergey), 5 (© Stacie
Stauff Smith Photography).

Cover photograph of green marble reproduced with
permission of istockphoto (© Milos Luzanin).

We would like to thank Ann Fullick for her invaluable help
in the preparation of this book.

Every effort has been made to contact copyright holders of
any material reproduced in this book. Any omissions will
be rectified in subsequent printings if notice is given to the
publisher.

Disclaimer
All the Internet addresses (URLs) given in this book were
valid at the time of going to press. However, due to the
dynamic nature of the Internet, some addresses may have
changed, or sites may have changed or ceased to exist since
publication. While the author and publisher regret any
inconvenience this may cause readers, no responsibility for
any such changes can be accepted by either the author or
the publisher.

Contents

Some words are shown in bold, **like this**. You can find out what they mean by looking in the glossary.

Glass All Around Us

▲ **Glass is strong enough to hold back tons of water!**

Glass is a strange and interesting material. It can be strong enough to hold back tons of water in an aquarium. It can be **fragile**, so that the slightest bump can cause the glass to break. Glass can be sharp enough to be used as a knife, or round and smooth like a paperweight.

Glass can allow light to pass through it, or it can be colored so dark that light is blocked. Glass reflects light, as in a mirror. It can also change light, as when light passes through a **prism** and creates a rainbow.

How is glass used?

You use glass every day. You drink out of a glass cup and look through a glass window. You look at yourself in a glass mirror or through eyeglasses that help you see more clearly. Glass stores food, holds perfume, and makes beautiful jewelry.

There are other ways glass is used that might surprise you. Ground glass is used to make bricks and highways. Water filters in fountains use **recycled** glass. **Fiberglass**, made from thin threads of glass, keeps homes warm or cool, makes sturdy boats, and helps form roof shingles. Ground glass or glass beads are used in artificial grass on sports fields. You will even find glass in the gravel in your goldfish's aquarium— and, of course, the aquarium itself can be glass.

Some uses of glass

We use glass in the following ways (and more):

- bathroom mirrors
- drinking glasses
- glass bricks
- golf course bunkers (sand traps)
- strong boats
- swimming pools
- water fountain filters
- windows.

▼ Glass can be as fragile as these glass ornaments.

A fulgurite is made of sand that has been struck by lightning.

Fulgur ✔

The word fulgurite comes from the Latin word *fulgur*, which means "lightning."

When lightning strikes

Nature is a skilled glassmaker. As a thunderstorm rolls along a coast, glass can form when lightning strikes sand. The electrical energy from lightning striking a sandy beach can measure up to 300 million **volts**. The air around the lightning is intensely hot—up to 30,000°C (54,000°F). It is so hot that it melts sand and forms glass.

Lightning glass is not exactly like the glass in a window or a bottle. This glass is called a **fulgurite**. It is shaped like a branch and can be up to 2 meters (6.5 feet) or so long. Fulgurites are hollow and glassy on the inside and sandy or gritty on the outside. When lightning strikes rock, it produces a different type of glass. A rock fulgurite has a shiny glass coating.

Lava glass

When a volcano erupts, it spews out lava, which produces a different type of natural glass. This glass, called **obsidian**, forms when lava cools so fast that **crystals** do not have time to grow. Obsidian is black, brown, or greenish and is quite useful for humans. Obsidian can be used for jewelry and for the knives doctors use in surgery, called **scalpels**.

▼ **This sharp arrowhead is made of obsidian.**

The edges of obsidian can be very sharp. The Aztec people (c. 1100–1519 CE), in present-day Mexico City, used those razor-sharp edges as teeth on swords and as knives. They also carved statues, beads, and jewelry from this shiny volcanic glass.

The History of Glass

▲ Egyptians made small bottles like these from colored glass.

There are several theories about how people learned to make glass, but there is no proof that any are correct. One popular idea is that, sometime between 5000 and 3500 BCE, **Phoenicians** traveling in ancient Syria stopped to cook dinner. The intense heat of the fire caused sand and other materials to melt and **fuse** together into glass.

By 3500 BCE, people in the Middle East were making glass beads. Remains of these beads have been found in present-day Egypt, Syria, Iraq, and Iran. By 1500 BCE, Egyptians and Syrians used shapes called **molds** to make glass bottles and jars.

By 1400 BCE, Egyptian glass artists were so skilled that they developed a type of **mosaic** glass now called **millefiori** (meaning "a thousand flowers" in Italian). A design was formed inside a thin rod of glass, much like a colored stick of hard candy. The rod was cut into discs, like tiny coins. The discs were arranged into a pattern, and more glass was used to glue the pattern together.

Bottle making

The next major advance in glassmaking was glassblowing, which began in about 30 BCE in Syria. Glass was melted in a **furnace** and gathered on the end of a metal tube. The artist blew steadily down the tube, creating a hollow form similar to a glass bubble. By 100 CE, the Romans blew glass into molds, which allowed glassmakers to make many bottles that were all the same size.

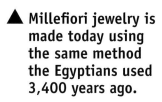

▲ Millefiori jewelry is made today using the same method the Egyptians used 3,400 years ago.

◀ Roman glass vases were blown into shape using molds.

9

Advances in glassmaking

By 1000 CE, European glassmakers were able to make flat sheet glass. **Molten** (hot, liquid) glass was poured onto a flat surface and rolled thin. Bubbles filled the glass and made it hard to see through.

In the 1200s, glass artists began creating pictures using colored glass. They built stunning stained glass windows for Europe's churches and cathedrals. They drew a pattern and cut glass pieces to match the pattern. They then connected the glass pieces using lead channels, called **cames**.

In the late 1400s, glassmakers in Venice, Italy, developed a perfectly clear, crystal-like glass, called *cristallo*. They used **quartz sand** (made of grains of ground rock) and a substance called **potash** to make brilliant, shining glass. Up until this time, most glass had a greenish tint because of the chemicals used.

▶ **Rose windows have thousands of pieces of colored glass.**

In the 1500s, colored glass was worth so much to West African tribes that they used glass beads for money. People there wore special beads to show their age, rank, wealth, and social status.

▲ Galileo could see four of Jupiter's moons with this telescope, made with a glass lens.

Galileo's stargazing

The Italian inventor Galileo developed an effective telescope using glass **lenses**. Galileo's telescope could see 20 times farther than the human eye, but it only focused on a small area. In 1610 Galileo became the first person to clearly see four of Jupiter's moons.

Lead glass, sheet glass

In 1674, in Great Britain, George Ravenscroft developed lead crystal by adding a chemical **compound** (mixture) called **lead oxide** to quartz sand and potash. This produced a bright, shining glass that could be cut and polished to make glass that shone like diamonds.

Mass-producing glass

Before the 1700s, glassmakers worked in factories, but an individual person made each piece. By the 1800s, during the Industrial Revolution, there was a change from handwork to machine work. As a result, glassmaking became a major industry.

▲ Built in 1851, London's Crystal Palace featured thousands of **panes** of glass.

People wanted window glass, called crown glass. Glassmakers started blowing molten glass into a cylinder. Once cooled, the glass was sliced down one side. When reheated, the cylinder flattened out as a large sheet of plate glass. Machines did the glass pressing and rolling, resulting in flatter glass with fewer bubbles.

Although machines could make flat glass, bottles and jars were still blown by hand. That changed in 1900, when U.S. glassmaker Michael Owens invented a glassblowing machine to make bottles. Owens's glassblowing machine produced 300 bottles in the time it took a human glassblower to make one bottle.

Using glass in the 1900s

In 1903 safety glass was invented. When struck, the glass did not break into sharp splinters that could cut people. Instead, the glass held together. Just over 20 years later, automakers begin using safety glass for windshields. Safety glass also became standard in many buildings.

In the 1930s, vision lenses improved with the introduction of trifocals. Trifocals have three lenses that let people see near, mid-range, and far away. Bifocals (two lenses—near and far) had been invented in 1784 by U.S. statesmen and inventor, Benjamin Franklin.

In the 1960s, scientists Elias Snitzer and J. W. Hicks discovered that they could direct a laser beam through a glass fiber. This was the start of **fiber optics**, the science of sending sound, light, and pictures over thin glass wires.

▼ Owens's glassblowing machine changed the glassmaking industry.

How Glass Is Made

▶ **Nearly three-fourths of glass is sand.**

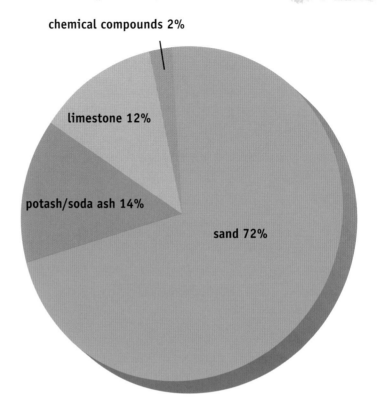

chemical compounds 2%

limestone 12%

potash/soda ash 14%

sand 72%

Making glass is much like making a cake. You collect the ingredients and mix them well. The major difference is in the heating. A household oven cannot produce the heat of a blast furnace.

Ingredients of glass

The basic ingredients in glass are **silica** from fine sand, potash or soda ash, and limestone. The materials have to be ground very fine before mixing. Glass artists make small batches of glass, while glass factories make glass by the ton. Companies make ordinary glass by mixing 72 percent white sand, 14 percent potash or soda ash, 12 percent limestone, and 2 percent chemical compounds (for color).

The color of the glass depends on the **elements** added to the glass mixture. For example, iron compounds make green or brownish glass. Cobalt makes blue glass. A gold compound makes a red glass.

A five-step process

There are five steps to making glass:

1. First, raw materials are melted in a furnace. Broken or waste glass, called **cullet**, is added to the furnace. A glass furnace heats at about 1,500°C (2,700°F).

2. Molten glass then needs to be refined, which means getting rid of gas bubbles that would weaken the finished glass.

3. The glass is poured into molds or blown into shapes.

4. Once in the required shape, the glass is heated and slowly cooled.

5. Finally, the glass is washed, cut, and polished.

Glass factory

A glass factory is divided into ends. The hot end is where the furnaces melt the glass. The cold end is where the glass is inspected for bubbles, cracks, or other problems.

▼ **Molten glass is blown into a shape.**

Using Glass

Glass production in the United States is a billion-dollar industry. There are several large manufacturers, hundreds of small shops, and more than 90,000 workers. But many glass manufacturers are moving their business to China.

▲ Float glass is used to make windows, like these panes.

Float glass

Float glass or window glass is a very flat, smooth glass used for windows. Glass manufacturers make float glass by pouring molten glass onto a bath of molten tin. The glass forms a floating ribbon and is smooth, flat, and thin. The glass moves through an oven called a **kiln**. Once cool and hard, the glass is cut into panes.

Optical glass

Optical glass is any glass used to help vision. The ingredients are measured precisely, and the heating must also be exact. The glass is made into a lens. The way the lens is cut and polished determines its use—whether it is for telescopes, microscopes, binoculars, camera lenses, or eyeglasses.

Leaded glass

Lead or leaded glass contains lead oxide in the glass mixture. This type of glass cracks easily and cannot stand heat. It does, however, make beautiful crystals. Leaded glass is ideal for chandeliers, inexpensive crystal jewelry, and crystal glasses. However, liquids left in lead crystal containers for a long period take in lead from the glass, which is harmful to people's health.

How a mirror is made

Your mirror is most likely made by laying down a thin layer of shiny aluminum against a piece of glass. The aluminum is attached to the glass and reflects light. The glass protects the aluminum from being scratched.

▼ **This glass lens lets you see a ladybug close-up.**

▲ Safety glass does not shatter into sharp pieces when it breaks.

Safety glass

Every car and truck has safety glass windows. Some safety glass is made by putting a thin layer of clear plastic between two layers of glass. If the glass breaks, the plastic holds the glass in place.

Another type of safety glass is **tempered** glass. Tempering means heating and cooling the glass to make it strong. If this glass breaks, it does not make sharp pieces. Instead, tempered glass breaks into small pebbles. Eyeglasses are made from tempered glass.

Most greenhouses are also made of safety glass. So are shower doors, cutting boards, and glass thermometers.

Borosilicate glass

Borosilicate glass gets its name from its two basic ingredients: borax and silica. This is strong glass that can be used for baking dishes, lightbulbs, and car headlights. Most glass used in science labs is borosilicate glass. Marbles are also made from borosilicate glass.

Fiberglass and foam glass

Invented in 1938, fiberglass is made from thin threads of glass. It is like cotton candy—light and airy. The fibers can be spun and stretched into threads that make **insulation**, which blocks heat or cold. Although fiberglass is lightweight, it is strong. It is also used to make hockey sticks, surfboards, and boats.

Heat resistant glass ✓

The glass on the underside of that National Aeronautics and Space Administration (NASA) space shuttle is special, heat-resistant glass. It must stand up against 1,260°C (2,300°F) temperatures. The glass is 93 percent air, which makes the tiles very lightweight. The air pockets protect the shuttle from heat.

▲ Lightbulbs, whether globes or spirals, are made from borosilicate glass.

Recycle!

▲ **All glass can be recycled.**

You finish up a jar of pickles or a bottle of juice. When you are done, you throw the glass away. Stop! Glass containers are 100 percent recyclable. You need to put that jar or bottle into a recycling bin.

Glass needs to be separated into clear, green, brown, and blue varieties. Clear glass is the most valuable. It can be used in any glass recycling process. Colored glass can only be used in producing the same colors—blue for blue, and so on. About 90 percent of recycled glass is used to make new glass containers. Today's spaghetti sauce jar may become tomorrow's perfume bottle.

Recycling saves

Most glass manufacturers rely on recycled glass for making new glass. Glass is collected, washed, and ground into cullet before being put in a furnace. Glass can be recycled repeatedly without losing quality.

Cullet is cheaper to use than the raw materials used to make glass. It takes less energy to **process** cullet because cullet melts at a lower temperature than raw materials used to make glass. Every 900 kilograms (1 ton) of recycled glass saves about 600 kilograms (1,300 pounds) of sand, 185 kilograms (410 pounds) of soda ash, 170 kilograms (380 pounds) of limestone, and 75 kilograms (160 pounds) of feldspar, a type of mineral. Recycling glass saves energy, raw materials, and money. It is good for the **environment** because it reduces the amount of glass waste.

▼ Recycled glass is collected, sorted, and washed. The clean glass is ground into cullet and heated. The hot, liquid glass is poured into molds and is used to make bottles again.

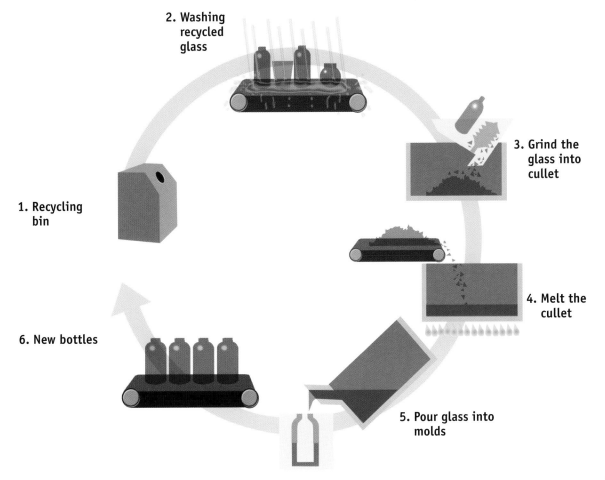

2. Washing recycled glass

3. Grind the glass into cullet

1. Recycling bin

4. Melt the cullet

6. New bottles

5. Pour glass into molds

▲ Recycled bottles
are sorted by color
and crushed.

International recycling

Recycling glass has become a global issue. The nation
with the greatest recycling rate is Japan, where homes
and businesses recycle every bit of waste possible.

In the United States, the glass recycling rate for bottles
and jars is only about 28 percent. Some states, however,
have higher recycling rates. California's glass recycling
rate is 79 percent of glass used.

In the **European Union**, more than 25 billion glass
bottles and jars are recycled every year. This works out
to about 12.7 million tons of glass collected throughout
Europe. British cities recycle only about 34 percent
of glass containers. That is far lower than Finland and
Switzerland, which both recycle more than 90 percent
of their glass containers.

Recycled glass products

Although much of the glass we recycle is used to produce new bottles and jars, recycled glass is not limited to this use. Fiberglass, used for insulating buildings and for building boats, is made of recycled glass fibers. Similar glass fibers are used to make fiber-optic cables for telephone and television lines.

Glass grit is part of the mixture used to blast dirt and soot from buildings. Recycled glass grit is also included when making the paint used to line roads and to paint bridges. Ceramic tiles, used in bathrooms, pools, kitchens, and entry halls, may also contain recycled glass. Wherever glass is used, recycled glass can also be used.

Saving energy

The energy saved from recycling a glass bottle can run a compact fluorescent lightbulb for 20 hours.

▼ **This clear aquarium gravel is made of glass.**

Glass Arts

▲ Glass can be used to make interesting outdoor sculptures.

Sun shines through a stained glass window, spreading a golden glow through a family kitchen. The doors to a seafood restaurant feature salmon leaping from a rushing stream that are **etched**, or cut, into the glass. A cut glass trophy, gleaming like diamonds, awaits the winner of a golf tournament. Sometimes, glass is more than bottles and jars. It is art glass.

Cloisonné

In **cloisonné** (pronounced "kloi-zuh-NAY"), an artist draws a pattern on paper. The artist transfers the pattern to pieces of metal. Thin metal wire is laid over the lines of the pattern and secured with something called soldering paste. The metal is placed in a kiln, where the wire pattern is fused to the metal.

Once the metal piece cools, the artist fills the cells (separated areas) formed by the wires with **frit**. Frit is colored glass crushed into powder. Mixed with water, the frit forms a paste. The artist uses the paste to fill the cells on the metal piece. The metal goes into the oven a second time. The frit melts into liquid glass that completely fills the cells. The finished piece is cooled and polished.

Cloisonné is popular in China, where it is used to make jewelry, beads, and ornaments. Small metal cloisonné boxes make beautiful gifts.

▼ **This is a cloisonné decorated egg.**

► Artists use acid cream to etch pictures or designs into glass.

Glass etching

Artists etch patterns onto windows, doors, mirrors, drinking glasses, and glass ornaments. The etching can be very large or small and detailed.

To etch glass, an artist draws a pattern on contact paper. The artist lays the contact paper on the glass and uses an art knife to cut out the pattern. Wearing gloves, the artist dabs etching cream on the glass. The cream contains acid that eats away at the glass. In about 5 to 15 minutes, the artist washes off the etching cream and peels off the contact paper. The design is permanently cut into the glass.

All glass is art

Glass has many uses. We use it in industry and in art. We make crystal vases to hold flowers and plain glasses from which to drink milk. We use glass lenses in microscopes and telescopes to make new discoveries. Some of us wear eyeglasses to see the print on this page.

All glass is art. Whether it is colored or crystal clear, there is beauty in glass. That beauty may be in a stained glass window or a Fabergé egg. It is also in the shards of sunlight winking through a glass window and in the reflections of ourselves as we glance in a mirror.

▼ **The prism breaks white light into the colors of a rainbow.**

Timeline

(These dates are often approximations.)

5000–3500 BCE
Phoenicians who are cooking on sand or forging metal discover how to produce glass.

500 MILLION YEARS AGO   **5000** BCE

1200s - 1300s
Stained glass is used to make beautiful cathedral windows.

1285
Salvino degli Armanti makes the first eyeglasses to correct vision.

1000
A technique is developed to roll flat sheet glass.

1000

late 1400s
Venetian glassmakers develop colorless, crystal-like glass, called *cristallo*, using quartz sand and potash.

1500

1827
Glass-pressing machines produce flat glass.

1800 ∿∿∿

1851
The Crystal Palace is built in Hyde Park, London.

1930s
Trifocals advance vision lenses.

1927
Automakers begin using safety glass for windshields.

1961
Elias Snitzer and J. W. Hicks direct a laser beam through a glass fiber.

1970
Corning Glass Works create optical fibers fine enough to be used commercially.

1980
A fiber optic cable links Boston and Washington, D.C., carrying a video signal.

∿∿∿ This symbol shows where there is a change of scale in the timeline or where a long period of time with no noted events has been left out.

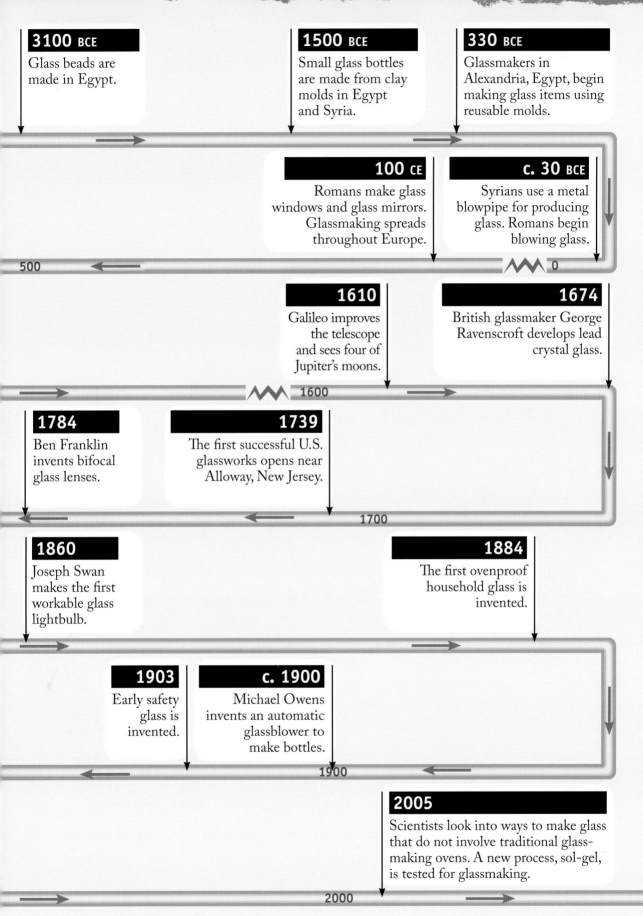

3100 BCE
Glass beads are made in Egypt.

1500 BCE
Small glass bottles are made from clay molds in Egypt and Syria.

330 BCE
Glassmakers in Alexandria, Egypt, begin making glass items using reusable molds.

100 CE
Romans make glass windows and glass mirrors. Glassmaking spreads throughout Europe.

c. 30 BCE
Syrians use a metal blowpipe for producing glass. Romans begin blowing glass.

500

0

1610
Galileo improves the telescope and sees four of Jupiter's moons.

1674
British glassmaker George Ravenscroft develops lead crystal glass.

1600

1784
Ben Franklin invents bifocal glass lenses.

1739
The first successful U.S. glassworks opens near Alloway, New Jersey.

1700

1860
Joseph Swan makes the first workable glass lightbulb.

1884
The first ovenproof household glass is invented.

1903
Early safety glass is invented.

c. 1900
Michael Owens invents an automatic glassblower to make bottles.

1900

2005
Scientists look into ways to make glass that do not involve traditional glass-making ovens. A new process, sol-gel, is tested for glassmaking.

2000

29

Glossary

blast furnace very hot oven used for melting glass

came lead channel used to connect stained glass pieces

cloisonné decorated with metal and glass

compound mixture made of two or more chemical elements

cristallo particularly clear form of glass

crystal clear mineral having a structure with angles and plane surfaces

cullet broken or waste glass suitable for melting again

element class of chemical substances that cannot be broken down into smaller substances

environment air, water, minerals, and living things in an area

etch cut or corrode with acid

European Union association of countries in Europe, formed in 1993

fiber optics use of light sent through glass fibers

fiberglass substance made of thin glass threads

fragile easily broken

frit basic material for making glass

fulgurite lightning glass

furnace apparatus for generating heat

fuse melt together

insulation material used to keep heat or cold in

kiln oven or furnace for drying, baking, or firing something, such as glass

lead oxide chemical compound of the elements lead and oxygen, it is used in making lead glass

lens piece of glass with one curved and one flat side

millefiori glasswork technique made by fusing discs of glass into a pattern

mold container for making a shape

molten made liquid by intense heat

mosaic picture made with small, colored pieces of glass, stone, or metal

obsidian volcanic glass

pane sheet of glass, usually a window

Phoenicians members of a culture that thrived in the Middle East around 1200 BCE to 332 BCE

potash compound of potassium carbonate or potassium oxide

prism clear piece of triangle-shaped glass that breaks up light passing through it

process actions for doing something

quartz sand granular material made from ground rock, which in this case is quartz (a compound of silicon and oxygen)

recycle renew, reuse, or process for another use

scalpel knife used in surgery

silica oxide of silicon, found in quartz sand, flint, and agate

temper treat with heat to harden

volt unit of electrical force

wavelength length of a wave cycle

Find Out More

Books

Fix, Alexandra. *Glass (Reduce, Reuse, Recycle)*. Chicago: Heinemann Library, 2008.

Stewart, Melissa. *How Does Sand Become Glass? (How Does It Happen?)*. Chicago: Raintree, 2010.

Williams, Brian. *The Science of a Pair of Glasses: The Science of Light.* Pleasantville, N.Y.: Gareth Stevens, 2009.

Websites

Glass Online: A Brief History of Glass
www.glassonline.com/infoserv/history.html
Visit the Glass Online website and learn more about glass history.

Recycling Glass
www.recycling-revolution.com/recycling-facts.html
www.green-networld.com/tips/glass.htm
Visit these websites to learn about recycling glass.

Places to visit

Fenton Art Glass Factory and Museum
420 Caroline Avenue
Williamstown, West Virginia 26187
(304) 375-7772
www.fentongiftshop.com/museum/Museum.htm
This museum is full of examples of glass from the Fenton Art Glass Company, and on select dates you can watch master craftspeople create art glass.

The Corning Museum of Glass
1 Museum Way
Corning, New York 14830
(607) 937-5371
www.cmog.org
This museum features regular glassblowing exhibitions as well as opportunities to see glassblowing in action.

Index